Conny Méndez

The Little
BLUE
BOOK

METAPHYSICS IN SIMPLE TERMS

ALIO Publishing Group

Contents

Contents

Disclaimer

Any metaphysical book should be read many times. Each time it is reread, it is better understood.

However… only that which is practiced remains with us. That which is only read, and not put into motion, goes away.

Introduction

This simple booklet is written in what this author calls "words of a penny". That is to say: in the simplest terms, with the intention of making it understandable to all those who need to know the truth of God, and do not have the knowledge with which to digest the texts of psychology and metaphysics, as they are written in Spanish.

Every time we hear or read something new, unknown to us, it awakens cells that were asleep in our brain. The second time we stumble upon that new idea, we understand it a little better. The cells start working on the idea. Soon after that, light is made in the mind, meaning: we accept the idea, adopt it, and put it into practice automatically.

This is how we awaken, learn, evolve, and advance. It is not necessary to make superhuman efforts to get things into our heads. It is a natural process. However, we must be willing to reread, reread, and reread again, until we feel that what we have learned is automatic. That is all.

Carry a copy of this booklet with you in your purse or pocket. Put another one on your bedside table. Reread it often, especially every time you have a problem; every time you are faced with a distressing or upsetting situation, whatever it may be.

Something amazing will happen to you, and that is that the booklet will open on the page you need to consult, and you will think it seems that this has been written for me.

Jesus Christ said: "In my Father's house, there are many mansions." Metaphysics is one of these mansions. Metaphysics is the study of mental and spiritual laws. It does not interfere with spiritualism, although that is another mansion in the Father's house.

May this little work bring you all the peace and prosperity which it has brought to so many others.

Blessings to you!

ONE: Dynamic Christianity

Before undertaking any trade, the candidate who is going to perform it receives instructions, or studies the technique of the same. However, there are those who undertake their task totally blind, without instructions...without technique...without compass – or design without notions of what they are going to find.

It is the human being who sets out on the task of living without even knowing what life is, without knowing why some lives are spent in opulence and satisfaction, while others are spent in misery and suffering. Some begin with all the advantages that affection can devise. And yet they are pursued by a shortcut of calamities.

And the human being struggles and conjectures, all erroneous, and the day of his death comes without his having even guessed the truth of it all. Learn a great truth: what you think, is manifested. Thoughts are things. It is your attitude that determines everything that happens to you.

Your own concept is what you see, not only in your body and character, but outwardly, in your living conditions in the material. Yes, it is just as you've read here. Thoughts are things. Now you will see that, if you are in the habit of thinking that you are of a healthy constitution, whatever you do, you will always be healthy.

Now suppose you were to change your way of thinking. If you allow yourself to be instilled with the fear of disease, and you begin to get sick, you lose your health. If you are born into wealth, you may always be wealthy – unless someone convinces you that destiny exists, and you start believing that yours can change according to bumps and setbacks, because you are believing it.

Your life – what happens to you – carries back your beliefs, and what you express with words. It is a law. It is a principle. Do you know what a principal is? It is an invariable law that never fails.

This law is called the Principle of Mentalism. If, in your mind is rooted the idea that:

accidents lie in wait for you at every step;

the infirmities of old age are inevitable; or

you are convinced you possess either bad luck, or good luck.

Whatever you normally expect, for better or worse...such will be the condition which you will see manifested in your life, and in everything you do. That is the reason for what happens to you.

You are never conscious of the ideas that fill your mind. They are formed according to what we are taught, or what we hear said.

As almost all of us are ignorant of the laws that govern life – the Laws of Creation – almost all of us spend our lives fabricating contrary conditions for ourselves. Observing this, one can clearly see how so many things which promised to be good, turn bad.

It is an inevitable effect of ignorant gropes, as if sailing blindly without map, rudder or compass; blaming our ills on life itself, and learning by rounds and rounds of blows, or attributing them to the will of the gods.

With what you have read so far, you may have realized that the human being is not what we have been led to believe. That is to say: a cork in the middle of the storm; tossed here and there, according to the waves. His life, his world, his circumstances – everything he is, and everything that happens to him, are his creations...and no one else's.

He is the king of his empire. He is the king of his empire...and if his opinion is precisely that he is merely a cork in the middle of a storm: so be it. He has believed it and allowed it. To be born with free will means to have been created with the individual right to choose.

Choose what? To think negatively, or positively. To be pessimistic, or optimistic. To think the ugly and the bad. What produces the ugly and the bad?

Or: to think the good and the beautiful; and what produces the good and the beautiful, outwardly or inwardly? Metaphysics has always taught that what we think often passes into the subconscious and settles there, acting as a reflection.

Modern psychology has only recently discovered it. When the human being is involved in the effects of his ignorance – that is to say, that he himself has provoked a calamity – he turns to God and begs Him to deliver him from suffering. Man sees that God sometimes attends to him, and that at other times, (inexplicably) He does not.

It is in the latter case that his relatives might console him by telling him that we must resign ourselves to God's will. In other words, everyone takes it for granted that the will of the Creator is evil. At the same time, religion teaches that God is our

Father: a Father of All loving-kindness and mercy. Do you see how these two theories do not agree?

Does it seem like common sense to you that an all loving, infinitely-wise Father could feel and express ill will towards His children? We mortal fathers and mothers could never attribute to any child the crimes we attribute to God. We would not be able to condemn to eternal fire, a creature of our blood for a natural fault of his mortal condition...and do we consider that God is capable?

That is to say, without our being clearly conscious of it, we are attributing to God the nature of a capricious and vengeful magnate, full of ill will, dependent on our least infractions to inflict on us punishments out of all proportion. It is natural to think this way.

When we are born, we live ignoring the rules and basic laws of life. We have already identified the reason for our calamities: we produce them with our thoughts. It is in this manner that we are made in the image and likeness of the Creator. We are creators. Creators, each of us, of our own manifestation.

Now then, why does it seem that God sometimes attends, and sometimes does not? You will see that prayer is the purest and highest thought that can be thought. It is polarizing the mind to the highest positive degree.

These are vibrations of light which we throw out when we pray; that is, when we think of God. These vibrations should instantly transform all the surrounding dark conditions into perfect and beautiful ones, as when a lamp is brought into a room which is in darkness.

Provided that the one who is praying thinks and believes that the God to whom he prays is a loving Father, who wishes to give all good to His child. In that case, God always attends. But how often, in general, mankind is in the habit of asking like this...

"Oh, Father God! Get me out of this predicament! I know you will think it isn't good for me, because you want to impose this test on me."

In other words, he has already denied any possibility of receiving it. He has more faith in that God who he was taught was capricious, vengeful, full of ill will, who only waits for us to commit the first infraction to inflict on us punishments of satanic cruelty. For he who asks, receives only according to his own image of God.

It is as simple as I tell you. Now, never again forget that God's will for you is good health, peace, happiness, well-being – all the good that He has created. Never again forget that God is neither the judge, nor the policeman, nor the executioner, nor the tyrant that you have been led to believe.

The truth is that He has created 7 laws – 7 principles that act in everything and always, and do not rest for a single minute. They are responsible for maintaining order and harmony throughout creation.

No policeman are needed in the spirit. He who does not march with the law, punishes himself. What you think is manifested; so learn to think correctly, and with the law, so that all the good that God wants for you is manifested.

St. Paul said that God is closer to us than our feet and our hands, and even closer than our breath. That's why we don't have to cry out to Him to be heard. It is enough to think a little of Him, so that what seems disordered, begins to recompose itself.

He has created us, and He knows us better than we know ourselves. He knows why we act this way or that way, and He does not expect us to behave like saints, when we are just learning to walk in this spiritual life.

I am going to beg you not to believe anything I am telling you without first checking it out. This is your divine and sovereign right.

Do not do what you have done up to now – accepting everything you hear and everything you see – without giving yourself the opportunity to judge between what is right and what is wrong.

TWO: The Mechanics of Thought

All day and all night long, we are thinking an infinite number of different things. A kind of constant cinematic movie, albeit disjointed, is always running through our mind. Among so many different ideas, we stop to contemplate, examine, or study some more than others. Why? Because they have stimulated our feelings.

They have produced in us a feeling of fear or antipathy, of sympathy, or pity; a feeling of liking or disliking – it does not matter. The fact is that, because of that feeling, the idea interests us. We review it later, and perhaps we discuss it with someone. This is meditating, and what is meditated upon passes into the subconscious, and is recorded there.

Once an idea is recorded in the subconscious, it becomes a reflex. You know that when the doctor taps you with some object in a particular area around your knee, your leg jumps. You have been touched in a sensitive spot, and you have reacted, haven't you?

In the same way, every time something happens in your life that refers to one of the ideas that are engraved in your subconscious, the reflex reacts in the exact way it was engraved. You adopt an attitude in accordance with the original feeling you felt when you first thought of that idea.

Metaphysicians call this a "concept" – that is: a belief, or conviction. The subconscious is not discerning. It does not decide anything. It does not have an opinion or think for itself. It has no power of protest. It has no will of its own. These are not its functions.

Its only function is to react by putting in order the reflex it has been given. It is in this sense, a wonderful filing cabinet, secretary, and an automatic librarian; one that does not rest, and can not fail. However, it does not have a sense of humor.

It does not know when an order has been given in jest, or in earnest. So if your nose is a bit bulging, and if you – to make others laugh – adopt a joke of calling it my stuffed potato nose, for example...as the subconscious is an exact servant, it has no sense of humor, and only knows how to obey unconditionally.

Then it will try, by all means, to fulfill the order given to it by your words and your feeling, and you will see how your nose looks more and more like a stuffed potato.

The word metaphysics means "beyond the physical" – that is, the science that studies and deals with everything that is invisible to the physical senses. It gives you the reason for all that we do not understand, for all that is mysterious; and it is exact, as you will see as you read this book.

Now try to recall the first time you heard the word "cold" mentioned. You were very small. Your elders said the word and taught you to fear it. By way of repetition, they taught you to understand it.

They told you not to get your feet wet; not to stand in a draft; not to approach someone because he had a cold and it would stick to him; etc; etc. All of this was recorded in the subconscious, and became a reflex.

You never had to remember the warnings of your elders. The damage was already done. From then on, your subconscious would give you a cold.

The best it could give you, every time you stood in a draft. Every time your feet got wet. Every time you came near a cold, and every time you heard there was a cold or flu epidemic.

Because of your elders, because of what you heard others say, because of what you have read in newspapers, and heard from advertisements on radio and television, and, above all: because you are ignorant of the metaphysical truth of life, you have accepted these erroneous ideas.

These have become reflexes which act without your premeditation automatically, and are the cause of all the ills which afflict you in the image of your life.

You have a bulky load of strange ideas which affect all departments of your life, your body, your soul, and your mind. Keep in mind that if you had not accepted them, if – by your right of free will to choose, accept, and reject – you had not accepted the negative, there is no germ, virus, or power in the world that could have attacked or convinced your subconscious to act in any other way than the one you gave it.

Your will, negative or positive, is the magnet that attracts to you the germs, the adverse circumstances, or the good ones. As we have already said: your attitude, negative or positive in the face of events, determines for you the effects.

THREE: The Infallible Formula

It turns out that every human mind contains an accumulation of opinions, convictions or misconceptions contrary to truth, and in conflict with the basic principles of creation, which are perennially manifested in external conditions.

This applies to all those calamities and sufferings which afflict man in the world in general: diseases, accidents, ailments, quarrels, dis-harmonies, deficiencies, failures, and even death. Happily, none of this conforms to the truth of being.

Fortunately, there is a way to erase all these false beliefs and replace them with correct ones, which will not only produce positive, good, happy, right conditions and circumstances...but once the error is corrected, and the truth is established in the subconscious, the negative things can never happen again in our lives.

The order has been changed. The magnet has changed its pole. It is absolutely impossible to attract anything that does not already find its correspondence in us. The infallible formula is the following:

every time something undesirable happens to you – that you get sick...that an accident happens to you...that you are robbed...that you are offended...that you are disturbed...if you are the cause of some evil to another or to yourself...

...if you are afflicted with a physical, moral or character defect...if you dislike someone...if you detest someone, or, if you love them too much and suffer for it...if you are tortured by jealousy...

...if you fall in love with someone who belongs to another...if you are the victim of injustice, or the victim of domination by another...

...the list is endless. So, tell yourself what condition is affecting you. Know the truth. Thus: Jesus Christ, the greatest of all masters of metaphysics, said "Know the truth, and it shall set you free."

Truth, the supreme law, is: perfect harmony, beauty, goodness, justice, freedom, health, intelligence, wisdom, love, and bliss. Anything contrary to this, is appearance. It is contrary to the supreme law of perfect harmony, and therefore is a lie, because it is contrary to truth.

Your higher Self is perfect, at this moment; and always has been perfect. It cannot get sick, because it is life. It cannot die for the same reason. It cannot grow old. It cannot suffer. It cannot fear. It is beautiful. It is love, intelligence, wisdom, and bliss. That is truth. It is your truth, mind, that of all human beings, and right now.

Not that the human being is God. Like a drop of seawater, it is not the sea...but it embraces all that forms and contains the sea, to an infinitesimal degree. And to an atom, that drop of water is a sea.

Whatever you are manifesting, anything that is happening to you that is contrary to perfect harmony, or anything that you yourself are doing or suffering that is contrary to perfect harmony, is due to an erroneous belief that you have created that you know.

Consequently, you are reflexively throwing outward and attracting its equal from the outside. It has nothing to do with your higher Self. It is still perfect. Your conditions and your situation are perfect.

Now, in each of the circumstances listed above, you must remember what I have just told you first of all; and then, say mentally or out loud, as you wish: "I do not accept it."

Say it firmly, but with infinite gentleness. Mental works do not need physical strength; neither thought nor spirit has muscles. When you say "I do not accept it", do it as if you were saying "I do not feel like it."

Say it calmly, but with the same conviction and firmness. Without shouting; without violence; without a movement; without abruptness. After you have said "I do not accept it", remember that your higher Self is perfect, and its conditions are perfect.

Now say: "I declare that the truth of this problem is: harmony, love, intelligence, justice, abundance, life, health, etc." Use whatever is the opposite of the negative condition which is manifesting at that moment. "Thank you Father, for You have heard me."

It will not do you any good to blindly believe what you've just read. You will have to check it out for yourself. In metaphysical language, this is called "the treatment." After any treatment, you have to maintain the attitude you have stated.

You cannot allow doubt to enter about the efficacy of the treatment. Nor can you re-express in words the concepts, opinions, and beliefs of before, because that destroys and nullifies the treatment.

The purpose is to transform the mental pattern which has been dominating in the subconscious. That is: the mental climate in which you have been living, with all your series of negative circumstances.

St. Paul said: "You are formed by the renewing of your mind." This renewal is done by changing every old belief as it comes before our life, or our conscience, in conscious disagreement with truth.

There are convictions that are so deeply rooted that they are what in metaphysical language are called crystallizations. These require more work than others, but every denial and affirmation made with respect to these crystallizations erases the original design, until it disappears completely, and nothing remains but truth.

You will see miracles occurring in your life, in your environment, and in your conditions.

You have no defects, but merely the appearance of defects. What you see as moral or physical defects are transitory, for as you know: the truth of your true Self – your Christ, your higher Self – is a perfect child of God, made in the likeness of the Father. The imperfections you are presenting to the world begin to fade away. It is a verifiable fact.

Any student of Christian metaphysics can corroborate what I have just told you. This is the great truth. Never forget it, and start practicing it now. The more you practice it, the more you will realize it, the more you will advance, and the happier you will feel.

Remember: you are unique, like your fingerprints. You were created by unique design, for a special purpose, that no one else but you can fulfill.

It has taken you 14,000 years to evolve to where you are today. God's expressions are infinite. You and I are only two of those infinite expressions. Your Christ is an intelligent being who loves you deliriously, and has been waiting for centuries for you to recognize Him.

The time has come. Speak to Him, ask Him, and wait for His answers. He is the only guide and master for you.

When you come to understand, accept and realize this truth, it will be the birth of Christ for you. This is what is prophesied for this age. He is the Messiah.

It is not that Jesus is born again now: it is that everyone will find the Christ in their consciousness, and in their heart; just as it happened to Jesus.

That is why he was called Jesus Christ.

FOUR: The Decree

Every word uttered is a decree that manifests itself outwardly. The word is the spoken thought. Jesus said two things which have not been taken seriously. One was: "By your words you will be condemned, and by your words you will be justified."

This does not mean that others will judge us by what we say. Although it is also true, as you have seen, that the master taught metaphysics, only that the race was not yet mature enough to understand it. On several occasions he warned that he still had many other things to say, but they could not be understood.

On other occasions, he said that "He who has ears to hear, let him hear." The second reference he made to the power of the word was: "It is not what goes into the mouth that defile a man, but what comes out of his mouth; for what comes out of the mouth, comes out of the heart."

It cannot be expressed more clearly. I propose that you pay attention to all that you decree in a single day. Let's recall a few from our collective past...

"Business is very bad."

"Things are very bad."

"The youth is lost."

"This traffic is impossible."

"Service is unbearable."

"You can't get service."

"Don't leave that there, or someone will steal it!"

"That corner is dangerous."

"I'm afraid to go out."

"Careful or you're going to fall."

"Watch out! You're going to get killed."

"You'll get run over by a car."

"You're going to break that."

"What bad luck I have."

"I can't eat that, it hurts."

"My bad memory"

"My allergy"

"My headache"

"My rheumatism"

"My bad digestion"

"That one over there is DEFINITELY a thief."

"I had no other choice."

Do not be surprised or complain, if by expressing it you see it happening. You have decreed it. You have given an order that must be carried out. Now remember and never forget: every word you utter is a decree, positive or negative.

If it is positive, it manifests in good. If it is negative, it manifests an evil. If it is against your neighbor, it is the same as if I decreed it against you; that is returned to you.

If it is kind and understanding towards others, you will receive kindness and understanding from others towards you. And when something annoying, negative, or unpleasant happens to you, do not say: "But I did not think or fear that this would happen to me."

You must have the sincerity and humility to try to remember in what terms you expressed yourself about another person. At the moment it came out of your heart, a very old concept rooted there; perhaps it is nothing more than a social custom like the generalities mentioned above, and one that you really do not wish to continue using.

As the feeling that accompanies a thought is what engraves it more firmly in the subconscious, the master Jesus, who never used superfluous words, expressed it very well when he said: "What comes out of the mouth comes out of the heart."

This gives us an unmistakable key to what we can do. It is in fact, the unequivocal key. The first feeling that teaches us, is fear. It is taught to us first by our parents, and then by our religious teachers.

When we feel fear, our heart races. We often say "my heart almost jumped out of my mouth" to show the degree of fear we feel at a given moment. Fear is what is behind all the negative phrases I quoted earlier.

St. Paul said we are transformed by the renewing of our mind. Every time you find yourself saying a negative phrase, you will know what kind of misconception you have ingrained in your subconscious, and you will know what kind of feeling it obeys.

The fear or lovelessness – cross it out; erase it by denying it as a liar, and affirm the truth if you do not want to continue manifesting it on the outside.

After a short time of this practice, you will notice that your speech is different. Your thinking is different. You, and your whole life, will be transformed by the renewal of your mind. When you are in meetings with other people, you will become perfectly aware of the kind of concepts they have, and you will notice them in everything that happens to them.

Whenever you hear negative conversations, do not affirm anything they express. Think: "I don't accept it for me, or for them." You don't have to tell them. It is better not to divulge the truth that you are learning; not because you have to hide it, but because there is an occult maxim that says "when the disciple is ready, the master appears."

By the law of attraction, everyone who is ready to go up a grade automatically approaches the one who can advance him, so don't try to be a catechist. Compel no one to receive lessons in the truth, for you may find that those whom you thought most willing, are the least sympathetic with it.

This is what Jesus meant when he said: "Give not that which is holy unto the dogs, neither cast your pearls before swine, lest they trample them under their feet, and turn and tear you in pieces."

FIVE: Does Faith Move Mountains?

Everyone knows the saying, and repeats it often. They repeat it like parrots because they do not really know what it means; nor why, nor how it is, that faith moves mountains. Few know that fear also moves mountains.

Fear and faith, are one and the same force. Fear is negative, and faith is positive.

Fear is faith in evil. That is: the conviction that bad things will happen. Faith is the conviction that what will happen is good, or that it will end well. Fear and faith are two sides of the same coin. Take a good look.

You never fear that something good will happen to you, nor do you ever say you have faith that bad things will happen to you. Faith is always associated with something we desire...and I don't think you desire evil for yourself. You fear it, don't you?

Whatever you fear you attract, and it happens to you. Now when it happens to you, you usually say with a triumphant air "Aha! I knew it. I felt it." And then you want to run off and repeat it, as if you wanted to show off your powers of clairvoyance. What actually happened is you thought it in fear.

Did you feel it? Of course you did. You felt it. You were saying it to yourself. You know that whatever is thought – feeling at the same time an emotion – is what manifests or attracts.

You anticipated it, and hoped for it. Anticipating and expecting is faith. Now notice that whatever you wait for with faith comes to you, and happens to you. So if you know this is so, what stops you from using faith for everything you desire: love, money, health, and so on?

It is a natural law. It is a divine ordinance. Christ taught it with the following words, which you know: "Whatsoever ye shall ask in prayer, believing, he shall receive." I did not invent that. It is in Matthew chapter 21, verse 22.

St. Mark expresses it even more clearly: "Whatever you ask for in prayer, you must believe that you will receive it, and it will be given to you." St. Paul says it with words that have no other interpretation: "Faith is the certainty of things hoped for, the conviction of things seen."

I have told you before that faith is the conviction of what is good. Now I will tell you that conviction comes from knowledge.

Suppose you live in a province, and you have never been to the capital. You want to go to the capital, and you take a train, car, or plane. You know where the capital is, and how to get there. One day you head for the capital, and you use whichever means of transportation suits you best...but on the way, you're not afraid of detouring to the moon, are you?

If you were a wild Indian, you would be trembling with fear, because you are totally unaware of what is happening to you. But, if you were a civilized person, you would go calmly, knowing that at such-and-such an hour, you will arrive at the capital. Ignorance of the principles of creation is what makes the world fear evil; not knowing how to use faith, or even what it is.

Faith is conviction assurance, but these have to be based on knowledge of something. You know that the capital exists, and that you are going towards it. That's why you know you won't end up on the moon. Now you know that when you desire something, if you fear not getting it, you will not get it.

If you deny it before you receive it – as demonstrated in the example given earlier with the prayer addressed to God by the generality of humans ("My God, grant me such a thing, although I know that you will not give it to me because you will think that it does not suit me") – you will not obtain it, because you have denied it beforehand. You have confessed that you do not expect it.

Let me give you the metaphysical formula to get what one desires. It is a formula to be used for everything. Try it for yourself. Do not blindly believe me.

"I desire such a thing in harmony for the whole world, and in accordance with the divine will; under grace, and in a perfect manner. Thank you Father, that you have heard me."

Now, do not hesitate for a moment. You have used the magic formula. You have fulfilled the whole law, and it will not be long before you will see your desire manifested.

Be patient. The longer you wait, the sooner you will see the result. In patience, tension and mental insistence destroy the treatment. The formula is what in metaphysics is called the treatment.

So that you will know what you have done by repeating the formula, I will explain the process in detail. By saying "in harmony for the whole world", you have eliminated all danger of your convenience harming others, just as it does not become possible for you to wish evil for another.

When you say "in accordance with the divine will", if what you wish is less-than-perfect for you, you will see that something much better happens than you expected.

In this case, it means that what you are wishing for was not going to be good enough, or was not going to be as good as you thought. God's will is perfect. When it says "under grace, and in a perfect way", it holds a wonderful secret.

But let me give you an example of what happens when you don't know how to ask under grace and in a perfect way:

A lady, in urgent need of a sum of money, asked for it on the 15th of every month. She had absolute faith that she would receive it, but her selfishness and indifference did not inspire her to ask for it with any consideration for others.

The next day, a car damaged her daughter, and on the 15th of the month. She received the exact amount she had asked for. It was paid by the insurance company for her daughter's accident. She asserted the law against herself.

To ask under grace and in a perfect manner, is to work with the spiritual law. The law of God, which always manifests itself on the spiritual plane.

There, on the spiritual plane, all is perfect without hindrance – without obstacle – **without hindrance** – without stumbling, or harm to anyone – without struggle or effort; smoothly, all with great love. And that is our truth.

That is the truth which, when known, sets us free. "Thank you Father, for you have heard me", is the highest expression of faith we can cherish. Jesus taught it and applied it to everything; from before breaking the bread, with which he fed 5,000, to telling how to turn the wine into his blood.

Giving thanks to the Father, before seeing the manifestation...as you will see, everything Jesus taught was metaphysical.

Whatever you desire – whatever you need – you can manifest. The Father has already foreseen everything. He has already given everything. But, you have to ask for it, as you feel the need.

You just have to remember: you cannot ask for evil for another, because that is returned to you, and whatever you ask for yourself. You must also ask for all mankind, because we are all children of the same Father.

For example: ask for great things. The Father is very rich, and He does not like stinginess. Don't say: "Daddy God, give me a little house. I only ask for a little house, even if it is small", when the reality is that you need a very big house because your family is big.

You will only receive what you ask for. Ask like this: "Father, give me and all mankind all the wonders of Your Kingdom." Now, make your list. To strengthen your faith, make a list of the things you want or need. List the objects or things.

Next to this list, make another list enumerating the things you wish to disappear, either in yourself or externally. On the same paper, write the formula I have given you above. Now read your paper every night, and do not allow yourself to feel the slightest doubt.

Give thanks again, every time you think about what you have written. When you see the things you have listed come to pass, cross them out; and at the end, when you see them all done, don't be so ungrateful as to think: "Maybe they were going to give them to me anyway", because that's a lie.

They were given to you because you asked for them correctly, and the outside accommodated to let them pass you by. Since you are already very accustomed to feeling fear, for various reasons, every time you find yourself attacked by a fear, repeat the following formula, which will erase the reflex you have engraved in your subconscious:

"I am not afraid. I do not want to be afraid. God is love, and in all creation. There is nothing to fear. I have faith. I want to feel faith."

A great master used to say: "The only thing to be afraid of is fear." You must repeat the formula, even when you tremble with terror. At that moment, all the more reason. Only the desire not to fear, and the desire to have faith, are sufficient to nullify all the effects of fear, and place us at the positive pole of faith.

I suppose you already know the psychological principle, which says that when one habit is erased, it must be replaced by another. Every time an idea crystallized in the subconscious is denied or rejected, it is erased a little.

The little vacuum thus created, must be immediately filled with an opposite idea. Otherwise, the vacuum will attract ideas of the same type, and which are always suspended in the atmosphere thought by others.

Little by little, you will see that your fears will disappear, if you have the will to be constant, repeating the formula in all circumstances that arise. Little by little, you will see that only the things you want to happen will happen to you. "By their fruits you shall know them", Jesus said.

This great instrument – the power of decree – is presented to us in that extraordinary account of creation found in the first two chapters of Genesis in the Bible. I suggest that you take some time to read this wonderful account.

As you read, you will realize that man – that is: you and I – was not created to be the fixture of circumstances, the victim of conditions, or a puppet moved by powers outside his domain.

On the contrary...we find that man occupies the pinnacle of creation. Far from being the most insignificant thing in the universe, he is – by the very nature of the powers given him by his Creator – the supreme authority appointed by God to rule the earth, and all created things.

Man is endowed with the same powers of the Creator, because he is made in His image and likeness. Man is the instrument through which the wisdom, love, life, and power of the Creative Spirit are expressed in fullness.

God placed man in a receptive and obedient universe, including his body, his affairs, his environment, who has no alternative but to carry into effect the edicts or decrees of his supreme authority.

The power to decree is absolute in man. The dominion God gave him is a revocable; and although the basic nature of the universe is good in the Creator's evaluation, it can appear to man only has he decrees it to appear.

We see that as long as man was obedient to his Creator, keeping his power to think and make decrees in tune with the spirit of Good [which is the structure of creation], he lived in a universe of good...a "Garden of Eden."

But when man fell, eating from the tree of the knowledge of good and evil, and chose to base his thinking in the use of his powers on good and evil, what as a free agent could he do? He immediately found sweat and thistles mixed with his daily bread.

Since the fall, man has been busy declaring his world good or evil, and his experiences have been in accordance with his decrees. This evidently shows how the universe responds, and how complete and far-reaching are man's dominion and authority.

SIX: Love.

This chapter is all that remains in order to complete your knowledge of the first principle of creation – the Principle of Mentalism, whose motto is: all is mind. Jesus Christ said: "Ye are Gods" in the Gospel of John chapter 10, verse 34.

Just as creation is all manifested thought, so man – who is a potential god – creates with thought all that he sees manifested, in equality and likeness with his Creator. This you have already learned.

You have also learned the mechanics of this mental creation. The character, positive or negative, of what you have created. The force, faith, or fear which determines the character.

The manner of changing the outward aspect of what you have created, denying and affirming. The power of the word, which is spoken thought, and which therefore confirms the orders you have given with your thoughts. And finally: the infallible formula for creating, manifesting and obtaining the best, the highest, the perfect: know the truth.

In obedience to the ordinance of master Jesus, you know that this truth is that we were created perfect by a perfect Creator, with the perfect essence of Himself; with free will to create positively or negatively. Therefore, evil is not a creation of God.

It has no power in the face of truth. It disappears by substituting it by the positive thought and word that

Jesus said: "Resist not evil." (Matthew chapter 5, verse 39.)

That is to say, that we dominate evil with good. The only truth is the good. From now on, you will never again be able to blame anyone for what happens to you. You will have to look yourself in the face and ask yourself:

"How was my mental state at that moment?"

"Was it positive or negative?"

"Did I feel faith, or fear?"

"What kind of decrees have I launched with my words?"

You will have to be honest and answer truthfully. Are you happy with what you are seeing...or do you dislike it?

In Christian metaphysics, we say that God has seven aspects: love, truth, life, intelligence, soul, spirit, and principal. You see, all these aspects are invisible states.

This means that everything is mental, so we cannot see or touch them. We feel and appreciate their effects. They exist, they act, they are real, they are things, and none of them can be denied. Love is called the character of God; the first aspect of God; the most potent of all forces; and, the most sensitive.

Few people know what love really is. Most believe that it is what is felt towards parents, children, spouses, lovers, etc. Affection, attraction, antipathy and hatred are different degrees of the same thing: feeling. Love is very complex, and cannot be defined with a single word, but collectively, love is understood as feeling.

Although this is nothing more than, so to speak, the outer edge of love, let us try to bring sensation as close as possible to love, in order to begin to understand it. The central point on the scale, which goes from hatred to feeling, and which we call love, is tolerance and goodwill.

It seems a contradiction, but when one loves too much or too little, tolerance and goodwill are lacking. When one hates, tolerance and goodwill are lacking. In other words, both excessive love and excessive un-love are the negation of tolerance and goodwill.

Jesus said: "Peace to men of goodwill." The implication is that anything beyond that does not bring peace. Peace is in the center: the perfect balance. Neither too much, nor too little.

And so in everything, all excesses – even an excess of good; excessive money; of love; of charity; of prayer; of sacrifice; etc. – unbalance the weight of the balance. They lean more to one side, and take away peace.

When Genesis says: "Of all the fruits of paradise you may eat, except of the fruit of the tree of the knowledge of good and evil", it refers precisely to that. The trunk of the tree symbolizes the center; the balance.

The branches start from that center, spread out to all sides, and produce fruits. Some manifest themselves as good; others, as evil. They symbolize the extremes.

You will see then that the forbidden fruit, which has caused so much tribulation in the world, is nothing other than the extremes, the excess in all aspects, since God, who created everything, declared good all his work.

Read it in Genesis, and observe that it only mentions the word evil with respect to the excess. I recommend you read and meditate on Ecclesiastes chapter 3, which tells us that everything has its time. Let us return to love.

Those mothers who say they love their children, who do not allow them to leave the nest, nor to marry, nor to act independently of them when they are already men and women of age, do not love.

They are selfish, and what they feel is a desire for possession. Those girlfriends and wives who suffer the tortures of jealousy? The same.

These types of love are nothing more than an excess of feeling. They exceed the measure, and therefore, go far beyond tolerance and goodwill. Excess of sentiment usually shows that there is a failure in the development of intelligence.

This will undoubtedly cause indignation in those people who fill their mouths, calling themselves "very sentimental." No one likes it when someone else discovers their lack of intelligence, but they can show it.

The excessive emotionality, like all excess, is bad. It is the proof that what counteracts it is missing. Excess heat, for example, is balanced by an equal amount of cold to make it bearable or unpleasant. Intelligence is cold. Emotion is warm.

A great emotional capacity is a magnificent and highly desirable quality, provided it is balanced by an equal intellectual capacity. This is what produces great artists; but the artist has his art in which to pour all his emotional strength.

On the other hand, the exaggeratedly-emotional person with little intellectual development, pours all his passion into the human beings around him, tries to bind them, and make them do his bidding.

The remedy against excessive emotionality is to think and reflect a lot, especially to meditate for a while, and daily, on intelligence. Start by asking oneself: "What does intelligence mean?"

Then continue by thinking that everything in the universe – plants, animals, etc. – contains intelligence.

Next, end by affirming: "I am intelligent, with the intelligence of God himself, since I have been created from the very essence of the Creator by intelligence, with intelligence, and from the intelligence of God."

Within a few days of repeating this treatment, you will already notice a change in elasticity, as well as in mental penetration. And after only one week of exercise, one can appreciate the transformation in the way of loving all others, a serenity, and a peculiar generosity, which one would never have believed oneself capable of expressing.

At the same time, one notices a total change in others towards oneself. This is because we are individuals, or indivisible; and what affects one, affects all. The step that one climbs helps the whole race.

We will now move on to deal with the number one enemy of all humanity: resentment and rancor...not to say hatred. There are hardly any human beings who are exempt from resentment, not knowing that it embitters the whole life, influences badly all the manifestations, and is the cause of all the disappointments that we suffer.

Even when we learn to deny and affirm, to know the truth, to watch and correct our thoughts and words...a single resentment, a grudge engraved in the subconscious and in the soul, acts like a small fountain of Gaul, which emanates its drop of bitterness, staining everything and surprisingly contradicting our greatest desires.

Nothing, not even the most perfect manifestation, can last as long as this infectious focus exists, spoiling our own being. The Bible, churches, and religions are tired of advocating forgiveness and love towards our enemies...and it is all in vain, as long as we are not taught the practical way to impose forgiveness towards those who hurt us.

It is often said: "I forgive, but I cannot forget." This is a lie. As long as one remembers an injury, one has not forgiven it.

We are going to give the infallible formula with which to forgive and forget, at the same time, for our own convenience. Since this establishes us in the central point of balance, that of tolerance and goodwill, and this effort is love.

St. John, the apostle of love, says: "Love is the fulfillment of the law." To fulfill the law of love is to fulfill all laws. It is to be with God, in God. It is to be happy; to feel satisfied and complete in all our manifestations.

My teacher used to say: "the man who loves well, is the most powerful man in the world." Here is the recipe to love well.

Every time you feel something unpleasant towards another person – or you find yourself resenting something that was done to you, or you recognize that you have an open resentment or desire for revenge – begin to deliberately remember this:

It's not about trying to forget what happened now. It's about remembering all the good things you know about that other person.

Try to relive the pleasant moments in which you enjoyed his company during times past, before the moment when he hurt you.

Insist on remembering the good things; their good qualities; the way you thought of them. If you manage to laugh at a joke he had told you, or at something funny you enjoyed together, the miracle is done. If a single treatment is not enough, repeat it as many times as necessary to erase resentment or rancor.

It is good that you do it up to 70 times. This is the fulfillment of the law given by Jesus: resist not evil. This is turning the other cheek. It is loving our enemies, blessing those who curse us, doing good to those who hate us, and praying for those who insult and persecute us, all without exposing ourselves to being trampled underfoot.

If you do it with sincerity, you will realize something very strange. And that is that: first, you will feel liberated; and then, that a mountain of small inconveniences that happen to you, and that you did not know what to attribute, disappear as if by enchantment, and your life goes on rails.

Moreover, you will feel loved by everyone, even by those people who didn't like you before. You will feel loved by everyone, even by those people you didn't like before.

What follows is that you learn to formulate your prayers – what in metaphysics we call treatments. As all day long we are thinking and decreeing, all day long we are praying negatively or positively, and creating our own conditions, states, and events. The important thing is to remain in the state of mind that the prayer expresses.

If after affirming, you allow yourself to return to the negative pole, you destroy the effect of the prayer. Watch your thoughts, and watch your words. Do not let yourself be carried away by what others express.

Remember that they ignore what you already know. Whatever you think and ask for yourself, think also for others.

We are all one in spirit, and that is the most effective way to give. Better than toys, treats and conveniences, for such perishable things tend to last only a few moments, while truth remains with the other forever.

Sooner or later, your spiritual gift will enter your conscious mind, and you will have done a saving work in a brother. The principle of rhythm, which is the law of the pendulum – the boomerang – returns to you the good you do, as well as the evil you do.

It has been said that one with God is the majority, so that a single person who raises his consciousness to the spiritual plane, and recognizes truth in the manner expressed above, is able to save an organization from ruin – to save a community, city or nation from any crisis – for it acts on the spiritual plane, which is truth, and truth dominates all the lower planes.

Know the truth and it shall set you free, in the face of sickness of self or other:

"I do not accept this appearance; neither for myself, nor for anyone else. I am life; in you, in me; in all the world. Thank you Father, because you have listened to me."

Repeat this affirmation every time that comes to your mind that case that forced you to express it, in every case of fear:

"I do not accept fear. God is love. I am his child. I am love. I am made of love, and by love. Thank you Father, that you have heard me. In every case of sadness of self or others, I do not accept it. I am joy; I am bliss."

Begin to list all the good things you have.

"Thank you Father. For any manifestation of scarcity, I do not accept this appearance. My world contains all, and I am the abundance of all. Thank you Father that today everything is covered in the face of all that is contrary to world or individual peace.

I do not accept this appearance of conflict. I am peace, harmony, and order. We are all one. Forgive them Father who know not what they do. I forgive all, and I forgive myself. Thank you Father, that you have heard me, and always hear me."

Of the metaphysics of the Ten Commandments, we insert here only two: the fifth, and the sixth. Among the laws called of God, which you will study when you feel like learning them, there is one called the law of correspondence.

It has nothing to do with letters or mail. Correspondence means, in this case, that which corresponds to something else that is equal to, as well as that which is equal too.

What does this mean? This law mandates that the conditions of each plane, or of each state of consciousness, are to be found repeated on all planes everywhere.

For example, we always want to know what the characteristics of "the beyond" are like, let's say. That "beyond" always refers to the plain above the earth, or to the plain below the earth. The model of this law is "as above, so below"; and, "as below, so above."

That is to say: just as on earth we have governments, schools, teachers, problems, and the way to solve them...there are hands, feet, ears, eyes; there are sounds, time space; there are flowers, as well as fruits.

In short, you know what is meant. In each plane and on every plane, there is what corresponds to all that, even if those other planes are invisible to our earthly eyes.

The only difference is, that as you ascend in the planes, the same conditions become less dense, more spacious, let's say "more pure; more beautiful; more interesting, but more complicated." This is because on each higher plane, there is one dimension more than on the previous one.

This does not mean that it is difficult for us to live in the new plane after leaving the old one. No: for the same reason that it is not more difficult for a child to walk only after he has learned that nothing bad will happen to him when he lets go.

Let us come to the point. The fifth commandment on earth says "Thou shalt not kill." This teaches us that we must not kill. You should not. But why is it wrong? No one really tells you; you simply must not kill.

Let's go to the plane of the beyond. There, the same law exists, only it says: "Thou shalt not kill...no matter how hard you try."

Not only will you not succeed, but since the instrument finds nothing to kill, it goes back where it came from. You threw it. It hurts you or hits you. That neither pleases you nor suits you, and you will not try again. You have already learned not to kill.

Now for the moment, let us study the sixth commandment: "Thou shalt not steal." It follows the same principle. On earth, we are taught not to steal. We are simply told it is wrong. This is not clear enough either.

And on the plane of the beyond, the commandment says: "Thou shalt not steal what does not belong to you." Don't even try; you can't. You can procure an equal object, but never the same one. It will not stay with you, and will return to its rightful owner.

On earth, these commandments seemed like prohibitions. On the next plane, they are revealed to you as conditions, laws, and principles which cannot be broken.

No one may kill you or steal from you. You may not kill anything or anyone. You may not appropriate what belongs to others, nor may anyone appropriate what belongs to you. But that is not the only happiness.

Take a good look. When on earth you are already incapable of killing or stealing, you are ready to learn the conditions of the other plane, which is called: of consciousness. That is to say, when you learn the first lesson, you go on to learn the second, correct?

That's true, but the great happiness is that when you learn the second lesson, it is not necessary that you have died, or that you are in the other plane beyond. No; you are alive and kicking here on earth.

You apply the second lesson, and you are amazed to see that this law works the same for you here on earth, as it does in heaven. That is, when you know that the truth is that no one can kill, and no one can steal, then no one will kill you, and no one can steal from you.

No one can take your car from your door, even if you leave the switch stuck. No one can rip your purse off your arm, or break into your house at night, or overcharge you. Nothing – nothing that is not honest, can happen to you.

What is yours, I ask? Yours, and no one else's. We are going to explain why this is so in the following paragraphs.

Why can't you kill? Because: life is just that. Life is not death. Life cannot die, for that would be a contradiction in terms. Life is eternally life, and can never be death. So, you say, what happens to me? I never die, since I am alive. Exactly.

You are in eternity, and no one can take your life away from you. Your life is God. Your life, is God's. Who takes away God's life?

That's why you can't kill anyone either. And he continues to live, more alive than ever on the other plane, just like you. Now, you know that what you do on earth is also returned to you.

Why? Because of the law of correspondence; because everything in one plane has its correspondence in the others. In all the others, this law says: "Do not do to others what you do not want others to do to you."

You know the reason. If you have not yet learned to obey this law, start observing how everything you do to others, in evil or in good, is returned to you. Now, why can't you steal? What makes this law work?

First, you will know that you have reached a dead end, if you have not yet resolved to accept the law of reincarnation. "Awww," you say, "what have we here?"

One of our metaphysical mottos is: "What you cannot accept, let it pass." But read on. If you don't like the idea, don't reincarnate; but you won't advance either.

You will remain stagnant, for the same reason that whoever does not want to accept that the sun will rise tomorrow will have to go into a closet every morning, and remain locked up there during all the hours of sunshine every day.

The law of evolution is an eternal experimentation in overcoming, as we have already seen above in the child who learns to walk, and who does not have to be afraid because he learns to let himself go. You know that everything changes from one thing to another, like the child who becomes a child; like the child who becomes a little turkey; like the little turkey who becomes an adult.

Then an old man, and then leaves the old shell here, and goes to look for a new one in the hereafter. When a being dies, he finds himself in the middle of a new set of circumstances in the beyond, but he has not lost anything of value, such as hearing, sight, feeling, will, free will, the faculty to move, to communicate with others, his identity, his "I".

On the contrary...since there is one more dimension, one sees more; hears more; feels more; understands more; embraces more; etc. In other words, nothing of what has been acquired can be lost. It is only adapted to the new conditions of the plane.

This means that on each plane, you acquire new, greater skills and knowledge. In each incarnated life, one acquires new experiences, and learns to use new objects and instruments which, although material here on earth, have their correspondence on the other invisible planes.

For what kind of advantage would it be to become a finished musician in the world, and not be able to externalize it on the next plane? And you have arrived at the great explanation:

What you acquire – you know, the instruments you have had to employ and learn to use, like cutlery, a bed, a match, etc. – on each plane, they have their correspondences. Don't forget!

And these, being already yours by right of conscience, as we say in metaphysics, appear automatically in your life or lives; one after the other, because you cannot be born in a family that does not have the means to provide you with what belongs to you, by right of conscience.

Many times it happens that a child comes into the world in a family lacking what belongs to him by right, and it turns out that soon the family acquires it, as if it were a great coincidence.

That is why you cannot steal what is yours...nor can you take possession of what you have not earned or surpassed in a previous life.

That is why the great happiness is knowing this law and these conditions. The law works on this earthly plane, and on all the other planes.

Therefore, you can be sure that no one can cause you losses, or take anything from you – not even your husband or your wife – as long as you have not done it to someone else.

So then: why be afraid? And if you have already learned that in this life, it is that you have it by right of conscience.

So the way to live happily is to learn the metaphysics of the Ten Commandments. With this small gift that we offer you, you will have put your foot on the first step of happiness. I will never tire of recommending that you constantly read this booklet.

Do not throw it in the drawer. Instead, keep it in your pocket, or purse, or backpack. Reread it every day, if you can. Put it into practice.

Remember its instructions; and, when you feel that the time has come to acquire more instruction, attend the appropriate lectures, and acquire the appropriate follow-up books. It will cost you nothing.

You will only pay for the books you wish to acquire, as they must be sold in order for them to continue circulating, for all who will benefit from finding them. Receive all our love.

May the light of your beloved presence of the I AM envelop you, fill you, illuminate you, guide you, and accompany you.

About the Author

Juana María de la Concepción Méndez Guzmán (Conny Méndez) was born in Caracas, Venezuela on April 11, 1898 to distinguished author and poet Eugenio Mendez y Mendoza, and Lastenia Guzman.

She devoted many years of her life to the theatre, as a producer, director, and actress in productions benefiting the International Red Cross Society during the years when the Society was under the direction of Chairwoman Doña Margarita de Guinand.

Her Musical output consists of more that forty compositions, the best known of which are in a folkloric vein and are still available in international record stores. Her classical and romantic works cover a wide range, including an Oratorio in the sacred tradition. She authored numerous poems, and performed at many international concerts that featured her own music.

Her spiritual works were largely influenced by Count Saint-Germain. In 1946, she founded the Christian Metaphysics Movement in Venezuela, and began to dedicate herself completely to this esoteric teaching, bringing her writings and lectures to the major cities of Central and South America.

The Venezuelan government has accorded her many high honors in recognition of her achievements, and she has been celebrated on numerous occasions for her artistic achievements.

She also enjoyed a generous level of recognition for her work in the field of Christian Metaphysics, with well-received works such as El Librito Azul (The Little Blue Book), Metafísica 4 en 1 (Power through Metaphysics), and El Maravilloso Número 7 (The Wonderful Number 7), among others.

Also By ALIO Publishing Group

The Hidden Secret of God: The Bible Decoded by Neville Goddard Volume 1

The Mystery of Christ: The Bible Decoded by Neville Goddard Volume 2

Meditation in 7 Pages: Reclaim Your Body, Renew Your Mind, and Raise Your Vibration using Short Simple Steps

Pay It Forward (and Back) A Gratitude Journal and Daily Planner to Attract Abundance

The Pineal Eye: Third Eye of Divine Mind

If I Knew Then What I Know Now...Real Life Lessons to Help You Live your Best Life

Occult Geometry and Hermetic Science of Motion and Number

How to Read The Tarot: A Key to the Wisdom of the Ages

Joseph Murphy and The Power of Your Mind (A 3 Book Set)

Succeed Using The Power of The Subconscious Mind in Business (with Obvious Adams)

The Science of Numerology for Beginners

Karmic Astrology: Mastering Key Life Lessons for All 12 Zodiac Signs

The Seven Main Aspects of God and The Ten Commandments: The Master Key to Life

Thought Conditioners. 40 Powerful Spiritual Phrases That Can Change The Quality of Your Life

For more information on past and future titles, visit us online at:

www.aliopublishing.com

www.ingramcontent.com/pod-product-compliance
Lightning Source LLC
Chambersburg PA
CBHW060401050426
42449CB00009B/1843